Back Pocket COACH

"We all have situations in our business lives when we wish we could call someone and get coached through the problem and best response. Back Pocket Coach does that, and helps prepare us ahead of time for situations that might arise."
— **Mary Adams,** Marketing Consultant

"Back Pocket Coach has created an archetypal language for business communication. It is an extraordinary achievement devastating in its simplicity. Since encountering Back Pocket Coach, I have found many occasions to use its strategies in my personal life. As a psychologist, I have found it helpful to teach my clients its language to manage problematic situations and conversations in their personal and professional lives, as well. I have even added Back Pocket Coach to my recommended reading list for clients."
— **F. D. Cameron,** Psy.D.

Back Pocket
COACH™

Back Pocket
COACH™

33 Effective Communication Strategies for Work & Life

Diane Brennan & Alexandra Ross

Books may be purchased in bulk by contacting
New View Press at:
CoachAlexandraRoss@gmail.com

Book Cover Design: NZ Graphics
Interior Design: WESType Publishing Services, Inc.
Graphic Designer: Dylan Matukaitis

ISBN 978-0-692-81715-5

Library of Congress Control Number: 2016919590
New View Press, Boulder, CO

1. Communication.   2. Leadership.   3. Business.

First Edition
Printed in the USA

*This book is dedicated to all of our clients
who had the courage to use these strategies and
who were able to make meaningful changes in
their lives and in the lives
of people they touched. You are the ones
who inspired us to write this book.
Thank you.*

Contents

Part Three
In Meetings

Part Four
Self-Reflection

Part Five
Situations and Issues   **45**

Part Six
Game Changing Conversations   69

Introduction

Have you ever been in a situation where having the right words to say could have made a big difference in the outcome of a conversation, but you couldn't articulate your thoughts? If so, welcome to the human experience.

This happens to all of us, which is what led us to develop *Back Pocket Coach: 33 Effective Communication Strategies for Work & Life.* These strategies are designed to support you in creating satisfying conversations that result in good outcomes.

We, Alexandra and Diane, have a collective total of more than 20,000 coaching conversations spanning 15+ years. These strategies include some of our favorite and most effective communication tips, along with some creative ways to use them.

This book is divided into six parts:

1. Strategies for One-on-One Conversations
2. Strategies for Conversations On-the-Fly
3. Strategies for In Meetings
4. Strategies for Self-Reflection
5. Suggested Strategies for Specific and Challenging Situations and Issues
6. Game Changing Conversations: Context & Methodology and Worksheet

Keep your *Back Pocket Coach* close, and use it regularly to support yourself in developing highly effective communication skills. With regular practice, you will be amazed by how quickly you will be having powerful conversations and achieving your desired outcomes.

The *Back Pocket Coach* print edition includes the Game Changing Conversations worksheet that is found in Part Six of this book. Download the 8.5″ x 11″ PDF worksheet at *www.BackPocketCoach.com*

How to Use
This Book

In this section, you'll find ideas to help you get the most from *Back Pocket Coach* strategies—whether you're an HR / organizational development professional, leader, manager or coach. We also talk about using these strategies in your personal life, because in the end, it's all personal. The best way to use these strategies is to just dive in and start experimenting to see what works best in a given situation.

Leaders and Managers

Being a leader or managing a team or project is challenging, period. With all that's happening around you it can be hard to think, and even harder to be clear and articulate in your communications. How often do you find yourself running from one meeting to another, answering questions, and juggling multiple priorities and people?

Back Pocket Coach's 33 strategies offer you a way to stop for a moment, reflect, refocus and find clarity for how to proceed. For example, Strategy #4: *Help me understand...* has multiple benefits including clarifying communications to avoid misunderstandings, quelling an emotional response and demonstrating that you value what others are thinking.

Strategy #6: *What are your expectations for...?* provides another way to gain understanding and ensure everyone is on the same page. These strategies support you in improving your communications, individually and with groups or teams.

You might try using strategies in meetings to expand thinking and encourage accountability. Here are two good ones: Strategy #22: *How does this relate to our bigger goal?* or Strategy #17: *Let's each summarize our actions and agreements.*

And for those times when you know that there's more to the story than what you're hearing, try using Strategy #23: *What are we thinking but not saying here?* This helps you create a safe environment while challenging the status quo. And it will allow you to engage participants in a meaningful way that helps move the team forward.

Back Pocket Coach will support you and your team in having better conversations and communications, which ultimately leads to achieving higher performance and results. While these strategies may not answer every concern, having *Back Pocket Coach* at your fingertips gives you access to strategic questions that can help you regroup and be articulate, even in the most challenging environments.

Talent Management, Organizational Development and Training

Do you want to be able to effectively attract and retain top talent? How about help leaders and teams ride the waves of organizational change and come through the process with a solid and optimistic path forward? These are examples of situations in which *Back Pocket Coach* can help.

Back Pocket Coach strategies can be a valuable resource to support your efforts in talent management, organizational development, and more. With scarce talent resources and work environments in a continuous state of flux, this is more important than ever.

Back Pocket Coach's 33 strategies can be used just-in-time to provide support for both individual and team challenges. And these same strategies can easily be developed into short, interactive training modules that will work with small teams from 10-15 people, or for much larger groups.

Say you have a team that needs some help with being more accountable—to each other and to their customer. You could choose the following three strategies and create a 90-minute interactive workshop: Strategy #5: *What is your understanding of our agreement?* Strategy #11: *Who is accountable?* And Strategy #12: *What expectations do you have of me?*

Or suppose you want to facilitate a workshop for managers to strengthen their skills in self-reflection and self-awareness. You could try a combination of: Strategy #28: *Notice and acknowledge successes.* Strategy #29: *What could I have done better or differently?* Or Strategy #30: *What am I learning?*

The possibilities are virtually limitless. *Back Pocket Coach* provides the strategy and the structure. You fill in the details to customize the training for your people and your environment.

Another way to use *Back Pocket Coach* is as a resource for your in-house coaching team. Your coaches can use every single one of these strategies for coaching their internal clients. These 33 strategies are backed by a depth of experience that can augment your in-house coaching team's expertise.

Back Pocket Coach will support your coaching team in delivering the best possible coaching service it can—and strengthen their coaching skills along the way.

Coaches

As coaches, we are lifelong learners. We truly enjoy our work, and we're always looking for resources to support our clients.

The 33 strategies you'll find in *Back Pocket Coach* evolved from our work with real clients facing real work and life challenges. If you're an experienced coach, you may even recognize some of the situations and issues from your own work. One strategy that's worth keeping top of mind to stay grounded, especially as you work in challenging environments, is Strategy #26: *Assume positive intent.* This serves as a good reminder to stay neutral and out of judgment with your clients and yourself.

For those newer to coaching, you might use *Back Pocket Coach* strategies in preparation for a coaching conversation. To help strengthen trust in your client and yourself, try Strategy #14: *Just keep breathing!* To replace judgment with inquiry, use Strategy #30: *What am I learning?* And to bring some lightness to your coaching presence, practice Strategy #33: *Shake it off!*

In Your Personal Life

We've given you some ideas for how to use *Back Pocket Coach* strategies in your professional life. By now, you might already have some ideas for how to apply them outside of work.

Strategy #1: *I would like to appreciate you for...* is one of our favorite all-around strategies. Research shows that wanting to be authentically appreciated tops people's list of what's important to them—more than money, fame or material goods.

So, when your partner goes out of their way to do something for you, or your friend stands by you in time of need, take a moment to acknowledge what it meant to you. If your child does something that warms your heart, tell him. Then observe how your message is received. Make authentic appreciation a habit and you will be amazed at how it will change your life and the lives of those around you.

Families have many of the same goals as teams. You want to be high functioning, you want to thrive, you want to have mutual respect and love for one another. So, many of the strategies that apply at work will apply at home. Take Strategy #7: *May I give you some feedback?* Instead of becoming angry or frustrated which can lead to conflict or avoidance, use this strategy to enter the conversation. We promise that you'll have a better outcome!

Two others you might try: Strategy #15: *May I make a request?* Whether you're asking your child to take out the trash or simply want to voice your request for the upcoming family vacation, this strategy will set the tone for a productive discussion. Strategy #25: *What if I don't have all the facts?* can also be helpful because it will help you stay curious and gather the facts, instead of assuming that you "know."

Try these and other *Back Pocket Coach* strategies for yourself, and share them with others. We hope you'll let us know what you learn!

PART ONE

One-on-One Conversations

Strategies for everyday situations that will help you be clear and authentic in all of your communications.

Strategies

1. I would like to appreciate you for...

2. What outcome do you want?

3. We both want the same thing here.

4. Help me understand...

5. What is your understanding of our agreement?

6. What are your expectations for...?

7. May I give you some feedback?

1

I would like to appreciate you for...

In appreciating others we acknowledge their value in the situation or relationship. Challenge yourself to notice what you can appreciate about someone, even if it's difficult. Try these simple guidelines:

1. Be **Authentic:** say specifically what their behavior or contribution meant to you

2. Be **Timely:** do it now

3. Make it a **Habit:** do it regularly.

STRATEGY

2

What outcome do you want?

This question allows you to focus on and articulate the desired outcome for the conversation, project or meeting. While it can be tempting to go off topic, it is more productive to be explicit and define the outcome so everyone is clear and can move toward the desired goal. Begin the conversation stating the goal. When ending, check for mutual understanding of what's occurred.

3

We both want
the same thing here.

It is challenging to get resolution when opinions seem far apart. One way to stay in the conversation is to find shared interest. If you have difficulty finding something you both want, step back and look at the big picture. Example, "I know you want this project to be successful. I want that, too." Both of you can regroup and work toward your common goal.

4

Help me understand...

You think you understand someone and later find you misinterpreted! "Help me understand" is a way of making sure you are both on the same page. It can also help you remain calm rather than be hijacked by an emotional reaction. For example: "Help me understand the purpose behind this process." "Help me understand" also lets the person know you value what he says.

5

What is your understanding of our agreement?

Clear agreements are central to success, both individually and in your work with others. How often have you thought you understood the task and upon presenting the finished product you learn it's not what your supervisor had in mind? Re-work is avoidable when there is mutual understanding of agreements. Don't wonder if you are on the same page. Ask the question!

6

What are your expectations for...?

People frequently operate from assumptions about expectations rather than fact. This limits success and leads to frustration. Clarifying expectations brings understanding of what is needed for getting started and achieving the final outcome. Asking the question lets others know your commitment to quality work. A dialogue on expectations engages both parties and sets a foundation for success.

7

May I give you some feedback?

We hear complaints about poor behavior, language, habits and performance concerns that are allowed to go on too long—hoping the situation will go away. When delivering feedback first ask the question, "May I give you some feedback?" This is a respectful way to get agreement to proceed, and it helps the person be more open to hearing what you have to say.

PART TWO

Conversations On-the-Fly

Someone catches you off guard or interrupts your flow with a comment or question. Try one of these strategies to stay clear and focused so you can respond with ease.

Strategies

8. Can we continue this conversation later?

9. Let me take some time to consider this.

10. What's the priority here?

11. Who is accountable?

12. What expectations do you have of me?

13. I may need to renegotiate our agreement.

14. Just keep breathing!

8

Can we continue this conversation later?

Have you ever been on a tight deadline when someone stops by to chat? Or, racing to your next meeting and someone stops you to ask a question? How do you excuse yourself gracefully? Try this: "I'd like to continue this conversation, and right now I'm on my way to a meeting" (or whatever is true). "When are you next available to talk?"

9

Let me take some time to consider this.

Don't say yes when you want to say no!
This can be detrimental to your health
and well-being—not to mention
impugn your credibility. When
someone puts you on the spot with a
request, it's natural to want to comply—
especially if it's your supervisor. Buying
yourself time and reflecting on whether
the request is realistic can keep you out
of a bind later.

10

What's the priority here?

This is a good question to keep in your back pocket—whether someone stops you in the hall for a conversation or stops by your office to talk. Any conversation can wander off topic. Wandering can be useful, but when allowed to continue for too long, the real priority gets lost. Asking, "What's the priority here?" helps everyone stay on point.

11

Who is accountable?

This simple yet powerful question can save you a lot of time and aggravation. It's not uncommon to find two people who both believe they are correct in understanding the accountability for a particular task. Imagine the surprise when learning each has an entirely different understanding! By asking, "Who is accountable?" everyone gets clarity up front.

12

What expectations do you have of me?

Whether we realize it or not, we all bring different expectations to the table. Instead of assuming you are both on the same page regarding, for example, who's going to do what by when, clarify! By asking this simple question, you are implicitly conveying your commitment and interest in being aligned with what needs to be done.

13

I may need to renegotiate our agreement.

Agreements are verbal contracts. It is best to agree only to what you know you can deliver. That said, sometimes an unforeseen conflict can make this impossible. Take action to renegotiate your agreement immediately! This gives the other person a chance to look for different options, and it preserves your standing as a person of integrity.

14

Just keep breathing!

Breathing with intention is a brilliantly simple way to get yourself out of your head and back into your body. It's a way to ground yourself, becoming more fully present. Do this: Stand or sit (feet on floor). Inhale slowly, focusing on the center of your chest; release the air slowly. Use it to relax and refresh right before you go into a high-stakes meeting or teleconference!

PART THREE

In Meetings

Strategies to help meetings get on track, stay on track, and generally be more effective.

Strategies

15. May I make a request?

16. I want to be sure we're clear. Will you please clarify…?

17. Let's each summarize our actions and agreements.

18. Please…let's not interrupt each other!

19. Hold that thought!

20. May I ask a question?

21. Time out!

22. How does this relate to our bigger goal?

23. What are we thinking but not saying here?

24. Be bold. Ask a question! Make a comment!

May I make a request?

This question serves many purposes: a request for clarification on a point; a request to go back to an agenda item; a request to cover a point not on the agenda; a request for action; or a request to park an item for later discussion. "May I make a request?" provides entry into a conversation already in progress.

16

I want to be sure we're clear. Will you please clarify...?

How many times have you walked away from a meeting confident you understood the conclusions or expected actions, only to later learn your interpretation was different from what others understood? This happens far more than you might think. Make sure everyone really is on the same page. Ask the question and get clarity before you leave the meeting.

17

Let's each summarize our actions and agreements.

Taking this action at every meeting strengthens awareness, accountability and forward movement. This is important because each of us views what happened anywhere from slightly differently to radically differently. Take 30 seconds to clarify each person's agreed actions. And remember to include by when with regard to completion dates.

18

Please...let's not interrupt each other!

Or: Please, let me finish! It is interesting to notice interruptions and how they impact our confidence and ability to intervene. Make this request when you experience one person interrupting another or if someone has interrupted you. Do it from strength, not drama. Listening and not interrupting each other during meetings is a wonderful operating agreement.

19

Hold that thought!

Someone introduces a new idea and suddenly the meeting is off-topic. Or, more than one idea is in play and focus is lost. "Hold that thought" is a respectful way to pause the action, communicate that you value what the speakers have to say, and refocus on the meeting's purpose. Try this: "Good point. Would you be willing to hold that thought and bring it up again after we resolve this current issue?"

20

May I ask a question?

This is a great way to refocus a meeting by referring to a topic that got sidetracked or was not fully explored. "May I ask a question?" implies your interest in someone's input. It allows you to enter the conversation as you "ask permission." It can also elicit participation from someone who has not yet spoken. Ask the question, then follow with, "I'd like to hear Bob's thoughts."

Time out!

Calling time out helps diffuse heated discussions. It's helpful for revisiting a point that was missed or glossed over, or when a lot of information has been put on the table. It's also effective in stopping people from talking over one another. Calling time out allows everyone time to regain objectivity, reflect and process information before moving on.

22

How does this relate to our bigger goal?

It's frustrating and wasteful for people to be in a meeting going nowhere. When we challenge ourselves to answer how the meeting objective relates to our bigger goal, we reconnect the group to shared purpose and back to a productive focus.

23

What are we thinking but not saying here?

Everyone is thinking about it, but no one is talking. We call this the elephant in the room. People may not have a safe or comfortable way to raise the subject. Asking this question with curiosity is a powerful way to begin a difficult conversation. Try it! It's non-confrontational, and has the added benefit of building trust along the way.

Be bold. Ask a question! Make a comment!

Fear of speaking up and being viewed as sounding stupid happens, no matter how smart or qualified we are. We have coached many truly brilliant people and, trust us, this is a universal human fear! Notice where or when you wanted to contribute. Ask a question or make a comment. Join the conversation and experience how freeing it can feel.

PART FOUR

Self-Reflection

Used regularly, these strategies will help you expand your self-awareness and more quickly build your skill set as an emotionally intelligent leader.

Strategies

25. What if I don't have all the facts?

26. Assume positive intent.

27. Who else needs to know or be included?

28. Notice and acknowledge successes.

29. What could I have done better or differently?

30. What am I learning?

31. What am I holding onto here?

32. Tell the truth respectfully.

33. Shake it off!

STRATEGY

25

What if I don't have all the facts?

Whether at work or in our personal lives, it is easy to make assumptions and fill in the blanks, thinking we know when we only imagine we know. This often leads to getting hijacked into emotional dramas, becoming a victim or blamer. Try this: Stay aware of what you know and what you don't know. Question your assumptions. Gather more information—then take action!

26

Assume positive intent.

Working with others can be challenging. Our emotions may cause us to question their intent or motivation, especially when they seem to be in opposition to ours. Next time, try this: Before assuming you "know" what the other person's intention is, ask! Then methodically reflect back what you heard them say. This simple act of clarifying will calm your nervous system and allow you to set the tone for a positive dialogue.

27

Who else needs to know or be included?

It is not uncommon to hold tightly to our responsibilities and limit the involvement of others, even when we could really use the help. Try this: Take a look at what you are accountable for. Ask yourself who else needs to know or be included. Including others appropriately can work wonders for your relationships. Remember to be clear about expectations and agreements for all.

28

Notice and acknowledge successes.

It's easy to rush through the days or weeks without noticing successes along the way. Make it a habit to reflect after a meeting or a challenging conversation. Do this privately and with your team. Take a few moments to notice what went well and appreciate your accomplishments. This practice is an opportunity to build on what you've learned. It also works wonders for morale!

29

What could I have done better or differently?

It is important to reflect on what you or the team might have done better. This is not about blaming yourself or anyone else; it is about reflecting—objectively and without judgment—on what you might do differently or fine-tune to improve results. Being able to look at yourself and take responsibility for your part in the process accelerates learning, individually and as a team.

30

What am I learning?

Make time to reflect on what you are learning—about yourself, the team, your supervisor, the customer and others. Become a reflective practitioner, able to be an observer of yourself and others without judgment. Try this: Pretend you are watching a movie, and you are one of the characters. Use a mindset of curiosity and explore what you notice and learn.

What am I holding onto here?

This question presents an opportunity to do a reality check. How are your tone, language and interactions with others? Are you visibly frustrated? Are you overly invested in an outcome? For example, holding rigidly to your point of view may put you at odds with others. It also sets you up to miss valuable information or input. Take action to let it go: Be curious, objective, open and willing to look at the bigger picture.

32

Tell the truth respectfully.

It is important to be able to speak your truth, and to do it in a way that respects rather than alienates others. If you communicate in a way that can be perceived as adversarial or confrontational, you could damage the relationship. Be clear, direct and deliver your message in a way that respects the dignity of others. This also gives you a much better chance of being heard.

33

Shake it off!

There will always be something that doesn't go your way. Keys to surviving and ultimately thriving: 1) don't take things personally; 2) stay focused on the outcome; 3) remain flexible. Not taking things personally is perhaps most critical. So when it feels like nothing is going your way, remember it is not all about you. So, shake it off!!

PART FIVE

Situations and Issues

Included in this section are some of the most common situations and issues we see people struggling with. Scan the list to see if one fits, then look at the suggested strategies for further guidance.

When you value someone's work or contribution

1. I would like to appreciate you for…
3. We both want the same thing here.
4. Help me understand…
28. Notice and acknowledge successes.

When the objective is unclear

2. What outcome do you want?

4. Help me understand…

6. What are your expectations for…?

10. What is the priority here?

12. What expectations do you have of me?

When you find yourself in disagreement with others

3. We both want the same thing here.

4. Help me understand…

5. What is your understanding of our agreement?

9. Let me take some time to consider this.

22. How does this relate to our bigger goal?

23. What are we thinking but not saying here?

25. What if I don't have all the facts?

26. Assume positive intent.

When you're just not connecting

4. Help me understand…

5. What is your understanding of our agreement?

16. I want to be sure we're clear. Will you please clarify…?

17. Let's each summarize our actions and agreements.

26. Assume positive intent.

To make sure you're on the same page

2. What outcome do you want?

4. Help me understand…

5. What is your understanding of our agreement?

6. What are your expectations for…?

10. What is the priority here?

12. What expectations do you have of me?

To avoid making assumptions

5. What is your understanding of our agreement?

11. Who is accountable?

17. Let's each summarize our actions and agreements.

26. Assume positive intent.

27. Who else needs to know or be included?

30. What am I learning?

How to diplomatically critique another

1. I would like to appreciate you for...

7. May I give you some feedback?

26. Assume positive intent.

32. Tell the truth respectfully.

When you need to buy time

8. Can we continue this conversation later?

9. Let me take some time to consider this.

19. Hold that thought!

When your role is unclear

2. What outcome do you want?

6. What are your expectations for…?

12. What expectations do you have of me?

20. May I ask a question?

22. How does this relate to our bigger goal?

When you can't deliver as promised

13. I may need to renegotiate our agreement.

27. Who else needs to know or be included?

29. What could I have done better or differently?

30. What am I learning?

32. Tell the truth respectfully.

When you're feeling overwhelmed

8. Can we continue this conversation later?

13. I may need to renegotiate our agreement.

14. Just keep breathing!

19. Hold that thought!

21. Time out!

30. What am I learning?

33. Shake it off!

How to step up when the situation calls for a leader

15. May I make a request?

16. I want to be sure we're clear. Will you please clarify…?

17. Let's each summarize our actions and agreements.

20. May I ask a question?

24. Be bold. Ask a question! Make a comment!

When the discussion gets heated

3. We both want the same thing here.

4. Help me understand…

18. Please…let's not interrupt each other.

26. Assume positive intent.

32. Tell the truth respectfully.

When everyone's talking at once

14. Just keep breathing!
18. Please…let's not interrupt each other!
19. Hold that thought!
20. May I ask a question?
21. Time out!

To get a meeting back on track

2. What outcome do you want?

10. What's the priority here?

11. Who is accountable?

15. May I make a request?

17. Let's each summarize our actions and agreements.

18. Please...let's not interrupt each other.

20. May I ask a question?

21. Time out!

22. How does this relate to our bigger goal?

When someone is rambling

10. What's the priority here?

15. May I make a request?

17. Let's each summarize our actions and agreements.

19. Hold that thought!

20. May I ask a question?

To make sure someone is ready to listen

1. I would like to appreciate you for…
7. May I give you some feedback?
20. May I ask a question?
26. Assume positive intent.

Making it safe
to speak the truth

1. I would like to appreciate you for...

3. We both want the same thing here.

4. Help me understand...

7. May I give you some feedback?

20. May I ask a question?

23. What are we thinking but not saying here?

31. What am I holding onto here?

32. Tell the truth respectfully.

Realize that your contribution is valuable

1. I would like to appreciate you for... (Practice self-appreciation.)

3. We both want the same thing here.

24. Be bold. Ask a question! Make a comment!

28. Notice and acknowledge successes.

When you're angry and think you have a reason to be

8. Can we continue this conversation later?

9. Let me take some time to consider this.

25. What if I don't have all the facts?

26. Assume positive intent.

29. What could I have done better or differently?

30. What am I learning?

31. What am I holding onto here?

33. Shake it off!

How to bring your "A" game every time

1. I would like to appreciate you for...
14. Just keep breathing!
28. Notice and acknowledge successes.
29. What could I have done better or differently?
30. What am I learning?
31. What am I holding onto here?
33. Shake it off!

When your ideas are met with resistance

15. May I make a request?

26. Assume positive intent.

30. What am I learning?

32. Tell the truth respectfully.

33. Shake it off!

PART SIX

Game Changing Conversations

The Game Changing Conversations' 8-step process prepares you for any difficult or high stakes conversation. Context and Methodology gives you insight and understanding for how to use the Worksheet. The Worksheet itself is a template you will use for thinking through challenges and creating a strategy that supports a successful outcome.

Game Changing Conversations Context and Methodology

Game Changing Conversations Worksheet

To download an 8.5" x 11" PDF of the Worksheet for Game Changing Conversations, please go to www.BackPocketCoach.com

CONTEXT AND METHODOLOGY FOR GAME CHANGING CONVERSATIONS

Here you will find a detailed explanation of the 8 steps in the Worksheet. Our purpose is to provide "the why" for recommended reflections, behaviors and actions because most of us learn better and retain more when we understand why we are doing something. If you are new to using the Worksheet, we recommend that you read through this Context and Methodology document, then refer back to it anytime you need a refresher.

IDENTIFY
my concern or challenge

It is important to get clarity on your presenting issue or concern. This will keep you from getting derailed or caught up in a different agenda or conversation. It is foundational for staying on track to achieve the outcome you want.

What's my
ROLE in this?

Difficult conversations can have a strong emotional charge. This is what makes it important to step back and view your situation objectively. Being willing to reflect on how you may have contributed to the current situation can take you off the defensive and give you a broader, more balanced perspective.

Ground yourself in
APPRECIATION

Authentic appreciation is incredibly powerful and is the number one thing people say they most need. We recommend that you start your conversation with something you appreciate about the other—even if it happens to be appreciating the difficulty of the situation. To get yourself into a good mindset, first reflect on what's working. Then speak your appreciation to the other person. It works wonders for setting a positive tone for the entire conversation.

Clarify the
goal or desired
OUTCOME

It is important to first identify what both parties want—and this may not be immediately obvious. So dig deep until you find it. Once you have it, articulate this collective interest to the other. You will be amazed at how powerful it can be to speak to what you both want.

EVALUATE
potential obstacles

Understanding the obstacles that might be in your way is essential to achieving your desired outcome. Don't miss this step! If you are working in a team environment, take advantage of that collective wisdom. Once you identify the obstacle, agree on a solution or mitigation. Then identify the task owner and deadline for resolution.

VISUALIZE
the end outcome

In this step, you will paint a vivid word picture of the outcome you are imagining and how good it will be when it comes to pass. You will share this with the other party and invite their thoughts and feedback. As you expand this vision together, seek to inspire everyone involved to enthusiastically embrace a unified way forward. We recommend spending some time developing this step, even writing it out in detail.

Make a
REQUEST

By now, there should be some consensus as to what is wanted—and maybe even some ideas for how to get there. One of the best ways to move the action forward is to make a concrete request for a next step. This could be as simple as asking to meet next Tuesday at 2:00 in your office—to define roles, to nail down deadlines and task owners, etc. Whatever it is, make it concrete. Give the other party the opportunity to make a request of you, too.

Emotional and mental
REHEARSAL

This is an incredibly important step that supercharges your ability to achieve any outcome. The reason it works is because you are aligning your emotional and mental "bodies" with the outcome you want. It also predisposes your nervous system to relax. When you are relaxed, you think more clearly.

Here's the process: In your mind's eye, simply imagine the end of the conversation as though your desired outcome has occurred. You might imagine feeling a spirit of goodwill in the room and being at ease with the other person. You could also imagine your relationship being stronger as a result of the conversation you just had. Or maybe it's simply a feeling of relief. Now feel the satisfaction of having achieved your outcome. And feel gratitude for this end result.

Practice emotional-mental rehearsal for 30 to 45 seconds before any important conversation or meeting—two to three times, if you can. Using this simple and powerful process will help you prime yourself for the best possible outcome available, for you and for everyone involved.

GAME CHANGING CONVERSATIONS WORKSHEET

1. IDENTIFY MY CONCERN OR CHALLENGE
Reflect on the situation and write a 1-2 sentence description of the concern or challenge.

2. WHAT'S MY ROLE IN THIS?
Reflect from a 30,000-foot view and identify: What part of this concern can I take responsibility for?

3. GROUND YOURSELF IN APPRECIATION
Reflect on what is working. Next, take action and speak to what you can appreciate about the other person or situation.

4. CLARIFY THE GOAL OR DESIRED OUTCOME
Reflect on what you both want. What do you want to accomplish together? Take action and articulate this collective interest to the other person.

5. EVALUATE POTENTIAL OBSTACLES
Reflect on what's in your way and how you can gain more perspective. Next, identify an action you can take to eliminate the obstacle and identify who can help you.

6. VISUALIZE THE DESIRED OUTCOME
Describe your vision for how the ideal scenario could unfold. Do it in such a way that inspires and motivates the other person to join you in moving toward this outcome together.

7. MAKE A REQUEST
Identify one concrete step that could move the action forward. Then make a request of the other person that is in line with this step—and/or offer to take an action yourself.

8. EMOTIONAL AND MENTAL REHEARSAL
Practice Emotional and Mental Rehearsal to help you imagine having achieved your desired outcome.

About the Authors

Alexandra Ross and Diane Brennan

Alexandra Ross coaches women in leadership, executives and teams in aerospace, technology, government and industry. Coaching since 1998, she brings over 25 years of business experience to every coaching conversation. Alexandra experienced the dynamics of moving from business owner to managing partner when she sold one of her companies. She often works with clients on the challenge of balancing power, effectiveness and authenticity within a corporate structure. Alexandra is an ICF Master Certified Coach.

Contact Alexandra at:

**CoachAlexandraRoss@gmail.com
or visit
www.CoachAlexandraRoss.com**

Diane Brennan is a coach and consultant, working with women in leadership, executives and teams in healthcare, aerospace, engineering and academics. She started coaching in 2000 and served as the President of the International Coach Federation in 2008. In addition to coaching, Diane has over 25 years of experience as a senior executive in private and publicly-traded healthcare organizations. She brings calm to the chaos in organizations and life.

Contact Diane at:

Diane@DianeBrennan.com
or visit
www.DianeBrennan.com

To work with Diane and Alexandra and bring the wisdom of these strategies to your organization, contact us at +1 303-284-3333.

Acknowledgments

Our work has been influenced by many leaders in the fields of business, organizational development, psychology and coaching. We would especially like to acknowledge our wonderful clients whom we've been honored to work with. We also want to acknowledge the many pioneers in organizational and leadership development and our colleagues who have contributed to our learning and life experiences.

Notes

Notes

Notes

Notes

Made in the USA
Lexington, KY
10 October 2017